Stella
and the
Dragon

Written by Jan Burchett and
Sara Vogler

Illustrated by Marcin Piwowarski

Collins

Stella and Frank are on a trip.

They see fantastic models.

Next, they turn scraps and junk into models.

"My dragon has black spots and jagged teeth," says Stella.

At night, they jump into beds.

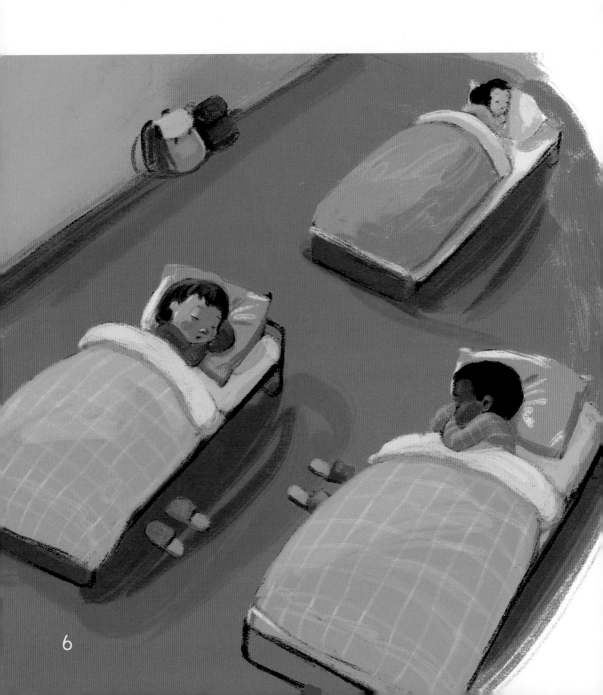

Thump! What was that?

"My dragon got bigger!..." says Stella.
It's grunting and swishing its tail.

Frank grabs Stella.
"Let's jump on its back," she says.

The dragon lifts into the air.
"Cling on tight!" yells Frank.

"What fun! Thank you, Dragon."

In the morning, the dragon is just a model.

It winks at Stella and Frank!

Night of the dragon

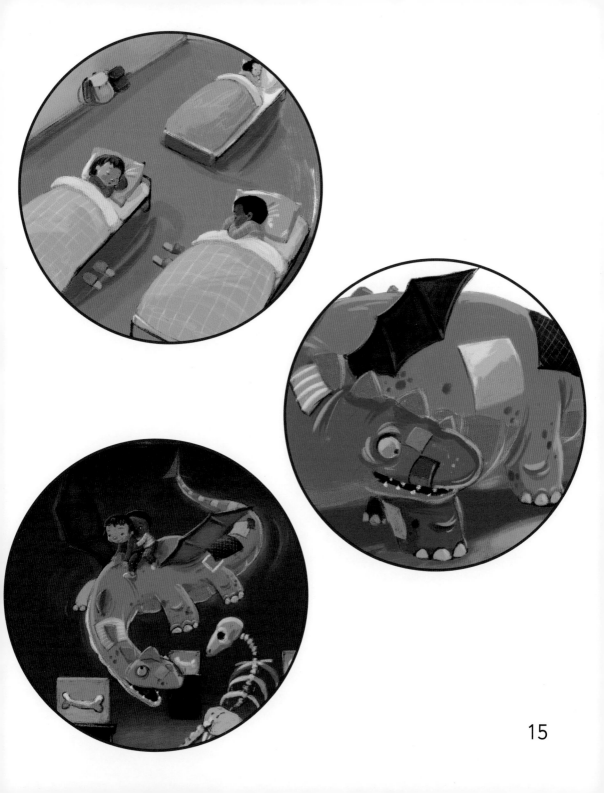

15

🐾 Review: After reading 🐾

Use your assessment from hearing the children read to choose any GPCs, words or tricky words that need additional practice.

Read 1: Decoding

- Turn to page 5 and ask: What sort of teeth has Stella made? (*jagged*) Ask the children: Can you explain what **jagged** means or draw a jagged shape in the air with your finger? (e.g. *an up and down/ragged/sharp shape*)

- Focus on words with adjacent consonants and short vowels.
  - o Point to **grunting** on page 8, and encourage them to sound out the phonemes. (g/r/u/n/t/i/ng)
  - o Repeat for the following on pages 8 and 9:

  Frank (F/r/a/nk/)   **grabs** (g/r/a/b/s)   **Stella** (S/t/e/ll/a)   **jump** (j/u/m/p)

- Model reading a page aloud, explaining that you are sounding the words out in your head as you go. Encourage the children to do the same. Say: Can you blend in your head when you read the words?

Read 2: Prosody

- Turn to page 10, and ask the children to find the exclamation mark. Point out how this shows what Stella's spoken words should be said with feeling. Encourage them to read Stella's words expressively – as if they are urgently yelling something important.

- On page 11, point out the comma to children. Explain that they need to pause for the comma. Encourage them to read the page, pausing at the comma.

Read 3: Comprehension

- Turn to the picture on page 10 and ask the children: Have you read or seen any stories about a dragon like this? What happened?

- Ask: Is the dragon just a model or alive – or both!? Let the children discuss this, and encourage them to back up their ideas by referring to the text. If necessary, remind them of the words **model** and **winks** on pages 12 and 13.

- Turn to pages 14 and 15 and ask the children Who? When? What? and Where? questions related to the pictures. For example ask:
  - o Where did the children go on a trip? (*a museum*)
  - o Where are they sleeping? (e.g. *in the museum, on camp beds*)
  - o What did they see? (*fantastic models*)
  - o Who rides on the dragon? (*Stella and Frank*)